Text and poems by R. P. Lister, wood-engravings by Miriam Macgregor

Foreword by Alan Titchmarsh

SILENT BOOKS

This edition published in Great Britain 1991, by
Silent Books, Swavesey, Cambridge CB4 5RA
First published by The Whittington Press 1985, in a limited edition of 250 copies.

ISBN 1 85183 025 1

Printed in Great Britain by St Edmundsbury Press,
Bury St Edmunds, Suffolk

ALLOTMENTS ARE SPECIAL TO ME, partly because my first gardening memory is of being walked among rows of sweet peas on my grandfather's allotment on the banks of the River Wharfe in Ilkey, Yorkshire.

There he grew the family's vegetables – early potatoes and tall peas, rhubarb that pushed its way through bottomless tin pails and blackberries that scrambled over old brass bedsteads.

In his black trilby, black waistcoat with gold watch chain. white collarless shirt with gold stud at the neck and baggy grey trousers, his leathery hand would lead me through sweet peas and wallflower plants, among cabbages and Brussels sprouts. And the sun always shone.

Twenty-five years later I acquired my own allotment in Berkshire, and discovered the joy of working alongside other like-minded gardeners who would travel the brief journey from home on their bikes with rake and spade and hoe strapped to the crossbar.

Allotment gardening brings out the basic instincts in man – to find a patch of land and to grow food to survive. It's a passion that still exists, even in this fast-moving age, and the slower pace combined with the succulence and flavour of the harvested crops has hooked me for life. Now I grow my vegetables on my own patch of ground, but the thrill of allotment gardening, and the frustration, and the graft, and the sweat, and the sheer unadulterated pleasure will never leave me.

ALAN TITCHMARSH

AN ALLOTMENT, says the dictionary, is a portion of a field assigned to a cottager to labour for himself; or a piece of ground let out for spare-time cultivation under a public scheme.

Early allotments were of the first kind. In the middle ages benevolent persons sometimes bequeathed patches of land to be cultivated by poor countrymen. Later, in the period of the enclosure of commons, cottagers were sometimes compensated for the loss of their rights to the common land by the 'allotment' of small areas of land, usually adjacent to the cottage. Allotments of this kind still exist. A group of country cottages with small or no attached gardens may have the right granted to them by the landowner to grow crops in the corner of an adjacent field. None of these usages, however, applied to the country as a whole or was widespread in any particular part of it. They all resulted merely from the charitable inclinations of individual landowners.

Allotments of the second kind – those let out for cultivation under a public scheme – came into being as a result of legislation towards the end of the last century and the beginning of this. The first serious attempt to provide allotments for the rural poor was made in the General Inclosure Act of 1845, but these were not intended to provide for 'non-agricultural labourers in towns'. Considerable resistance to such schemes was encountered, particularly in the early years, from farmers and landowners, since it was thought that allotting land for the use of the labouring classes would make them too independent. They would expend on their allotments energies that ought to be reserved exclusively for their employers; and, being tied down to a piece of land in which they had invested time and labour to produce food for themselves, they would be less willing to uproot themselves and move elsewhere according to the shifts in demand for paid labour. Nevertheless, gradual progress was made, partly as a result of the extension of the franchise, which placed in the hands of humbler voters a power which they slowly learned to use. Compulsory powers of acquiring land for allotments were granted to local authorities by the Allotment Act of 1887; the Small Holdings and Allotment Acts of 1907 and 1908 provided the legal structure on which the modern allotments system is based.

These measures were at first intended principally to benefit impoverished rural labourers, but during the First World
War the demand for allotments in urban areas increased
dramatically. There was an urgent need to produce more
home-grown food to compensate for the shortages of im-
ported food resulting from the U-boat attacks on shipping.

The smoke of autumn, and the autumn gale
Blowing the leaves across the sun,
The staked-up flowers,
All tell a tale:
After the labour and the plodding hours
The season's nearly done.

The old tower, now, has seen it all before,
A thousand times, or thereabouts.
Plenty and dearth,
And peace and war:
People have had their faith, and had their doubts,
But you can trust the earth.

Turn it well over, scatter the seeds,
It'll yield something that a fellow needs . . .
And feed the centipedes.

Beaten by rain and bashed about by wind,
  Nipped by the frost or buried by the snows,
Drab, dogged and undisciplined,
  The cabbage grows.

Beside your average herbaceous border,
  Or sentimental pansies neatly spaced,
The cabbage is a picture of disorder
  In dubious taste.

And yet it has a beauty of its own.
  The poet, gazing sullenly upon it,
Has hardly ever, with a soulful groan,
  Written a sonnet,

Even a limping and lop-sided one.
And yet why not? Surely it could be done?

The Defence of the Realm Act of 1916 empowered local authorities to requisition for this purpose any small piece of open space, including parks, playing fields and tracts of un-developed building land. The number of allotments more than doubled during this period, rising from 600,000 in 1913 to 1,500,000 in 1918.

After the war the demand for allotments declined, but it soon revived again in the slump of the twenties and early thirties. By 1939 there were some 740,000 individual allot-ments in England and Wales (about 570,000 in urban areas and 170,000 in rural areas). On the outbreak of the Second World War further powers were given to local councils to obtain land for allotments. In 1940, after Dunkirk, the need for home-grown food became even more desperate; the Dig for Victory campaign stimulated still further the demand for allotments, and by the end of 1942 there were once again, as in 1918, about a million and a half allotments in England and Wales. In 1944 it was estimated that 10 per cent of the food produced in this country was grown on allotments, in private gardens and on plots of land culti-vated by service personnel.

On winter afternoons I often go
Past the allotments in the snow.
Beyond the huts, beyond the spire,
The downs rise high and bleak and cold.
I think that I am feeling old,
I shall go home and sit by the fire.

A brave man with a strange machine,
Who on a fearful day of storm
Is seen to go
Pushing that strange machine along the row
And back again.
And every now and then a bean
Drops through the riddle (or the screen)
Into the hole prepared for it,
Where it will snugly fit.
He does not care for wind or rain,
He will fulfil his self-appointed norm.
Each bean will find its place,
And there's no need to stoop and sow,
Only to push this strange contraption to and fro,
This strange creation of the human brain.
Indomitable is the human race,
Boundless the human wit.
Only the rain has quenched the cigarette he lit.

After the second war, as after the first, the demand for allotments again declined. In the following years it has fluctuated, for a variety of reasons. The question naturally arises: why, in the present age, do people want allotments at all? The desperate rural poverty that called them up in

I sometimes think that never blooms so green
The cauliflower as where a lot of junk has been
Gathered into a heap and rotted down
And buried deep to do its work unseen.

They say that strong men have been known to keep
Their weary and their suffering wives from sleep
As through the night they trundle endless loads
To an imaginary compost-heap.

Come, fill a barrow to the brim, and fling
Its contents on this heap; for by the spring
It will have rotted down to some extent.
If not, then keep it till the following.

Up from earth's surface in a messy pile
The compost rises up; after a while
It rots, and on its wealth the produce grows,
But ah! the stink of it is sometimes vile.

the first place is to a large extent a thing of the past; a much smaller proportion of the 'non-agricultural labourers in towns' who were not supposed to benefit from the earlier schemes lives on the edge of the breadline now than in the hungry eighteen-forties. A national need for home-grown food is still less a feature of the present day. Yet the demand for allotments continues and appears to be by now a permanent feature of the national life.

One reason certainly is that it is still – or can be – cheaper to grow food than to buy it. Among the ten or twenty per cent of our population who are still really under-privileged, a markedly higher standard of living can be attained by the cultivation of an allotment. For both the rural and the urban poor, now as before, the staple crop on an allotment is usually the potato, which provides a solid basis for a diet limited at the luxury end. For the less heavily disadvantaged considerable savings can still be made by growing the vegetables that form such an expensive item of the standard national diet: cabbages, cauliflowers, peas, beans, carrots, Brussels sprouts. Moving up the financial scale, those in more comfortable income groups can still make appreciable

economies by growing their own marrows, cucumbers, rad-
ishes, lettuce, tomatoes, spinach; the list can be extended,
and, if cultivation under glass is included, can cover a range
of exotic products such as the aubergine, the pimento, okra
etc. There are more special crops that may be grown for
economic or other reasons: tobacco, which is widely seen on
allotments; and, no doubt, cannabis, if one took a little
trouble to search for it. And then in allotments where people

The caterpillar of the cabbage white
Feasts upon cabbages by day and night,
Thereby reducing them, like tired old souls,
To stubborn residues joined up by holes.
Wherefore the grower views them with distaste,
Seeing his hours of labour run to waste,
His sought-for produce turned to butterflies
Taking to wing upon the summer skies.

of West Indian origin hold a proportion of the plots, the number devoted exclusively to sweet corn is noticeable.

But shortage of means is not the only motivation of the allotment-holder, and is probably in most cases not the principal one. The motive of many can be summed up in the word 'escape'. For some – perhaps overwhelmingly for the less prosperous industrial worker – going home from work means a transition from tedious labour in dreary surroundings to cramped accommodation, fractious children and a careworn, nagging wife. There are two escapes: the pub, which is agreeable but costs money, and the allotment, which is agreeable in a quite different way and saves it.

The element of escape is not always so desperate but may still be present. The urban worker with a harmonious domestic life may still find in his allotment a lung, a haven where he and sometimes his wife as well perform soothing labours in the fresh air. The mean streets are mostly not quite so mean as they were in the last century or even in the thirties; but mean they still are, and even the bean-rows, compost-heaps and tottering hutments of the allotment area are still an attractive contrast to acres of brick and slate.

Thistle, ragwort, dandelion,
These shall have no place in Zion:
No fate has the ground elder earned
But to be carted off and burned.
Chickweed, avaunt! Begone, fat hen!
Burdock, vacate the plots of men!
Nettle and couch-grass, come not here!
Buttercup, buttercup, draw not near!
Weedkiller, slug-bait, netting and spray
Take up the half of the digalong day.

As I was saying, things like dogs and cats
And field mice and rats
And pigeons and slugs
And small boys and bugs,
These are your regular raiders;
But then you get the strange invaders,
Such as a bunch of cows
Breaking in for a bit of a browse
Like a battalion of tanks,
And not a word of thanks,
But down with the cabbages and the beans.
Next time it'll be machines
From outer space
Coming to obliterate the human race
And pick up anything they can snatch.
I bet they start off with my patch,
And I hope that chap Don
Still laughs his head off as he looks on.

Lettuces, half rotten,
Papers in between.
Such a sight, once seen
Or smelt, never forgotten.

Huts sag; roofs must be mended.
Neighbours consulted, and they view
The damage. Patch it, renew it?
Herself, below, instructs them what to do,
Knowing how badly, after all, they'll do it.
A woman's work is never ended.

But the relief of poverty and the need for escape may be less important motives than the sheer deep-rooted urge to grow things. It is an instinct widely spread in the human race and is by repute particularly strong in the English people, even more so than in the British as a whole. It may be that the English, industrialised for so long, have a particular yearning for the rural life of the romantic imagination. It is certainly true that many allotment holders are neither poor nor afflicted by a cramped or inharmonious home environment. Quite an appreciable proportion of them, in the years since the war, have been most emphatically of the middle class, and some even of the more prosperous end of that class. They can afford to buy any vegetables they want, without making sacrifices in the way of clothes or holidays; they have comfortable homes and, quite often, gardens to grow flowers in and lawns on which to take their leisure in the sun. Yet they toil in their allotments to grow the vegetables they could quite easily buy. Often they rationalise it, claiming that the peas, beans, parsnips or broccoli straight out of their allotment are immensely tastier and more nourishing than those bought in the shops, which have

suffered from a long journey to market and a long sojourn on the vegetable counter. This is true enough, and it is also true that they gain the sheer pleasure of exercising in the fresh air the muscles which so often atrophy in the office, and of seeing their own sustenance emerging in an ever-miraculous manner from the soil. All the same, excellent

This, say the cats, is Our Patch.
So they behave in the traditional manner.
Odd, while the people are growing beans,
The toms are chasing the queens,
Spraying the borders of the domain
And generally raising Cain,
Not giving a tinker's curse
For all the people; not even knowing
Why they're there and what they're growing.

In the wet wet wet
There's nothing like a mug of tea:
Forget
The world, feel free;
There's all the time yet
For doing; time to be.

reasons though these may be, it is difficult to avoid the con-
clusion that the middle classes enjoy digging in their allotments because they are, or like to think they are, simple
country folk at heart.

  If the web of causes that takes people to their allotments

is a complex one, the scene that awaits them there is no less so. For this is a whole sub-culture, the allotment society: and like other cultural groups it shows a great diversity within itself and at the same time exhibits to the outside observer some marked similarities in its features. Nobody, on perceiving an allotment area from a train or car, ever took it for anything else; it is instantly recognisable. Always there are the same scruffy huts; the same bean-rows; the same air of semi-dereliction, of haphazardness, of a messiness bordering on the sordid; the same paths criss-crossing between the patches; the neat rows in one patch and the sprawling weeds in another. Men, and fewer women, can be seen working here and there, stooped over the soil, leaning on spade or fork, pushing barrows from one place to another, or apparently lost in contemplation. There are the same piles of thrown-out leaves and stalks; the same lines of dangling objects, possibly intended to scare away the birds.

Look more closely, and this apparent uniformity turns into a quite extravagant diversity, involving every possible variant of human eccentricity and idiosyncrasy. The huts are astonishing assemblages of diverse materials; among them railway sleepers, corrugated iron, tarpaulin, miscellaneous planking, plastic sheeting and what may be called Bits Found in Skips figure largely. Some huts are cosily domestic, featuring glazed windows and curtains; others are

A miracle of rare device,
Seen perhaps once, but rarely twice.
Close your eyes with holy dread
And weave a circle round it thrice,
For from such miracles are fed
The compost-heaps of Paradise.

Here he is among his mealies,
And looking, as he should, at home.
The sun's not quite as warm
As it might be, for this crop,
But it grows all right, given care,
In the variable English air.
Fortune, whose wheel is
A whit haphazard in its ways,
Carries us here and there,
And when the gales of history drop
A man wakes up and finds he's growing maize
In Bucks or Yorks or Wilts, on his off days.
Whatever the deal is,
A wise man takes the hand he's dealt, and plays.
One time blown west across the foam,
Once more blown east, and then the storm
Dies down: the mud of England goes
Creeping between the African toes.

bleak. Most are flanked by a number of oil drums, these being a prominent feature of allotments. The construction of compost-heaps is one of the most variable features; a kind of wire basket is fairly common, though corrugated iron and assemblages of nailed-together timbers also feature largely. Here it is worth noting that there are those to whom the compost-heap is of supreme importance, yet others simply do not bother about compost-heaps at all. And then there are the extraordinary makeshift bits of apparatus contrived by the allotment-holders to serve as barrows, seeding-machines, and tool-chests; all evidence of human ingenuity exercised with loving care to mould the minute rural estates nearer to the occupier's ideal.

The greatest variety however is in the allotment-holders themselves. They may look drab and uniform to the casual onlooker; drab they may be, but uniform they are not. There are the enclosers, those who jealously fence in everything that can conceivably be fenced; the builders, thwarted architects whose huts seem sometimes more important to them than their plots. There are those who limit themselves to one spade, one hoe and one rake; they are often, though

Why do you always grow more than you need?
You sow and you dig and you weed
And all the rest of it,
And where does it all lead?
It sprouts, it grows, and then it runs to seed,
And the bugs and the bacteria get the best of it.

not always, the ones who live nearby and carry their tools down to their patch on their shoulders. Others come on scooters or in cars; some build great chests, with giant padlocks, on their allotments to house a remarkable collection of equipment, tools, buckets, bottles, bowls, plastic sheeting, roofing felt, the odd child's wooden railway engine or Christmas tree. . . . There are the orderly, the disorganised, the laborious, the lazy, the experts, the simpletons, the practical, the philosophers, the experimenters and the traditionalists; those who grow whatever vegetable is latest in fashion, and those who stick to the tried and trusted; the enthusiasts for organic materials and those who favour chemicals.

And will allotments survive? One tenant of a London suburban allotment painted a gloomy picture. In the mid-seventies, she said, there had been a move towards self-sufficiency and the waiting-list for an allotment in this area was eighteen months to two years. Currently the council cannot get rid of all the plots. The allotments being worked tend to be those nearer the gate of entry or in the middle of the area, leaving unused allotments as a border round

And do the window-glasses
Make the lettuces grow?
The old men say it must be so:
And only the old men know.

You may have noticed: there are those
   Who know exactly what you ought to do.
   They tell you, too,
In matchless prose,
Laying down all the laws
   According to the learned books.
   Reminds me of when a lot of rooks
Fly up in circles, arguing the caws;
It sort of grates upon the ear.
   I don't deny he's very likely right,
   And it's a sorry sight,
Offends him, being near,
My patch; so rank
   Sometimes you'd say it's mostly weed,
   And the mosquitoes breed
In the old tank,
Enough to make a man despair.

the other three sides. There is a gradual falling away of older people, who in their more vigorous days may have worked as many as three plots, but now cut their efforts down to working only two and finally one.

So are allotments on their way out? It is safe to say that, barring some exceptionally misguided measure of government economy, they are not. While a patch of ground is available for people to grow vegetables on, they will grow vegetables on it. More of them may wish to do so at one time than at another, according to the country's economic state, the distribution or maldistribution of wealth, the whim of taste or fashion; but it is highly probable that the patch of worked allotments in the centre of my friend's plots, like all the worked patches in all the other areas up and down the country, is even now creeping back towards the edges, swallowing up the unused allotments on its way. No one can forecast the future course of things, but it would be surprising if the proportion of worked allotments did not increase rather than diminish in the remaining years of this century.

There's no denying the beauty of the day
And life in general. There's the communion
Of soul with soul, that's most important. Hey,
And a touch of casual disorder; take a gun
And shoot down any line that's straight: it's out
Of place in this most natural world. Things
Are not to be despised; the only doubt
Is monetary value, that's what brings
Confusion, contempt, corruption into the scene.
But worthless things are priceless . . . as is praise;
Rest after effort, that's an evergreen
Recipe for content and length of days;
And air, the good air, not only fresh but free.
Ultimate luxury: a mug of tea.

The flowers that once I plucked for you
Were cabbage, onion, pea and bean.
All these in my allotment grew,
With marigold and feverfew,
Gromwell, and various kinds of spurge.
But in my precious leisure hours
I picked these vegetable flowers
And, with a dim primeval urge,
Presented them to you, my queen.
How green! you murmured. Ah, how green!
And, with your eyes all wet with dew,
Propelled me gently from the scene.

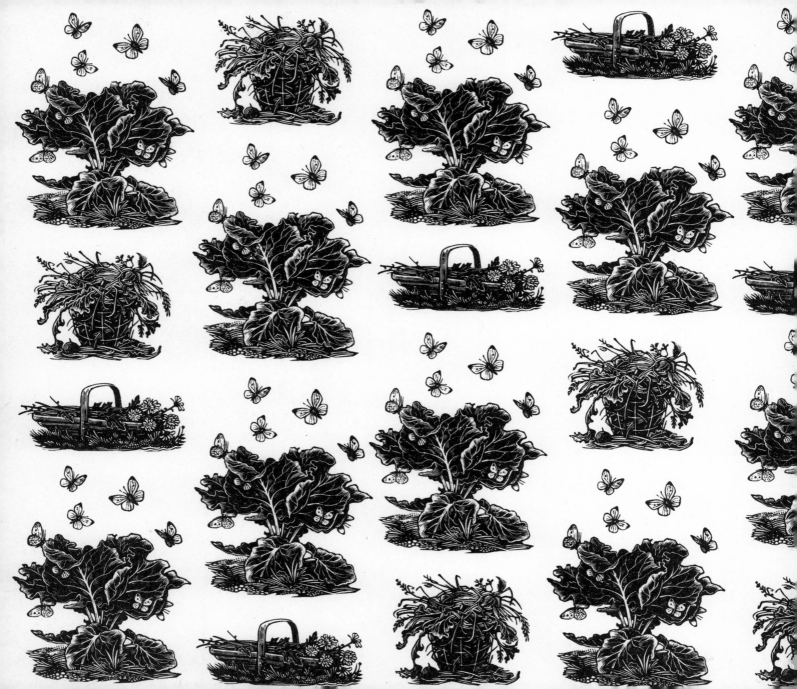